T0193146

a box of longing
with fifty drawers

A Box of Longing
With Fifty Drawers

Jen Benka

Soft Skull Press
Brooklyn, NY 2005

ACKNOWLEDGMENTS

An earlier version of this manuscript was published as a limited edition artist book by the Booklyn Artists Alliance, Brooklyn, NY, 2003, under the title, *A Revisioning of the Preamble to the Constitution of the United States of America*. Mark Wagner, designer.

Several poems in this collection were published by belladonna books, Brooklyn, NY, 2003, as *belladonna #51*, a chaplet. Erica Kaufman, curator. Rachel Levitsky, editor.

Individual poems were published on cafemo.com and failbetter.com.

The writing of this manuscript was made possible in part by a poetry fellowship from the Wisconsin Arts Board.

I am grateful to the many artists, activists and writers who made space for this work: Antler, Maggie Balistreri, everyone at Booklyn, Cindia Cameron, Cathy Cook, Bill Dempsey, Kris Dresen, Nick Frank, Veronica Golos, Bob Holman, Meg Kearney, Anne Kingsbury & Karl Gartung, Jennifer Knox, Ada Limon, Brendan Lorber, Pamela Means, Antonio Merenda, Daniel Nester, Kristin Prevallet, Jenny Runde, Sabley Sabin & Cathy Arney, Stacy Szymaszek, Angelo Verga, Mark Wagner, Terry Wit, Woodland Pattern Book Center, and my family.

Thanks to Soft Skull, especially Shanna Compton, Tennessee Jones, and Richard Eoin Nash.

This is your country, your laconism.
Your indifference and your emotion.

So much life for just one homeland.
So much death for just one dictionary.

— *Adam Zagajewski*

The paper is covered with indelible letters that
no one spoke, that no one dictated, that have
fallen there and ignite and burn and go out...
Everywhere solitary prisoners begin to create
the words of the new dialogue.

— *Octavio Paz*

CONTENTS

WE

where were we during the convening
two hundred years ago or yesterday
we, not of planter class, but mud hands digging
where were we during the convening
our work, these words, are missing
the tired, the poor, waylaid
where were we during the convening
two hundred years ago or yesterday.

THE

the days wave into months
the sickness claims too many
the bodies overboard
the thick mist finally lifts
the sight of land at last.

PEOPLE

crushed dust thrown
across ocean
family bones
a name, my own.

OF

of ambush of going into hiding of this walk
of the confusion of the alienation
of the existence of things impossible
of failure (or success)
of the woods of water of rocks
of catacombs of my scream (with no echo)
of the passing hours of childhood
of bark (scribbled with words)
of the mirror of me of a translucent temple
of approval of an insatiable audience
of prey of the flames of these rituals
of all this
of our hearts
of love of darkness
of the cosmos.

Note: This poem was made by abstracting and
recording in sequence phrases that began with the
word "of" from ten poems by Urszula Benka pub-
lished in *Young Poets of a New Poland* (Forest
Books, 1993).

THE

first word
long line
lost bird

the

last time
strange dream
white lie

the

steel beam
black coal
blue steam

the

clay bowl
tall grass
dyed wool

the

thin glass
bread crumb
first blast

the

day's done
young son
war's won.

UNITED

to stand alone together.

STATES

this land has no name
not taken, thieves
tracing rivers and t-squares
more borders.

IN

this is the side no one sees
behind the thin of skin.

ORDER

as	if
it	were
a	game
they	played
mapping	us
neatly	into
tidy	towns
collected	in
civil	states
ready	for
the	bidding.

TO

the trajectory of giving:

a cable strung between two points—

a gondola dangling

waits for feeling / the chain reaction / locomotion

carry this there.

FORM

tin cup filled
with tepid tap
water that tastes
like sulfur even in glass.

A

shapeless breath begins
the beginning of the next
breath before a word

MORE

spindly stems stand in sand
night blooming cereus
smuggles water and waits
for the dark to flower.

PERFECT

he took it apart
convinced that he could fix it
but staring at the pieces
spread out across the table
he knew it was now
impossible to repair.

UNION

locked link
a line of strangers
hoping for the other's kindness
inevitably have to defend themselves.

ESTABLISH

all things made with mindfulness of meaningful legacy.

JUSTICE

one theory suggests
that all theories
in their translation to practice
rely on innocent people
to pay the price for progress.

INSURE

safe in the deep of warm underwater
the moon makes sense
rapture in waves of spring salt
carried back to land
the legacy of love
and where it began.

DOMESTIC

the porcelain plate tips
falls to the floor and smashes.
she picks up the pieces, cuts her hand
and hurries to clean the mess
so the mistress will never know she bled
red like the flames from a burning bush
or a book of dreams where the first sentence reads
no one has to wait for freedom.

TRANQUILITY

where language meets silence
slow on the sleepy page
and love and love and love
hushes into dreaming.

PROVIDE

what can I hope to give you
what was I given to give
fifty-two words
before a few thousand more
the structure for a story
an heirloom
the best that money could buy.

FOR

used to indicate the purpose of an action
tongue turning touching tongue
gentle kiss leading lips
used to indicate a destination
warm wet wide
used to indicate the object of desire
hip lift and tempting
slowly slide inside
deeper in to the perfect dark.

THE

this that the
the that and this
this and that the the
this and that the the

this that the
the that and this
this and that the the
this and that the the

this this this this that
this this this this that
this this this this that
this this this this that

that that that the
that that that the
that that that the

the that the this the that the this
the that the this the that the this
the this and that
the this and that

and the and the and the and the and the and the
and this and this and this and this
and that and this
and this and that

this that the
the that and this
this and that the the
this and that the the

this that the
the that and this
this and that the the
this and that the the

the the
the the
the the
the the.

COMMON

to share something
but never meet.

DEFENSE

of the people
1861

to repel
invasions and suppress
insurrections

by the people
1865

all able-bodied men
between the ages
of eighteen and forty-five
are liable
for service

for the people

war may be declared
by a simple resolution
of both houses and approval
by the President

600,000

young men lost.

PROMOTE

permeate this invisible cell.
introduce a new species of
thought.
encourage replication.
hope for critical mass.

THE

begin
    here
        then
           keep
                moving to the right.

GENERAL

vague ideas become
obtuse sentences become
contradictory instructions become
improperly installed parts become
flawed constructions become
collapse.

WELFARE

she sits on her stoop
says just wait when summer comes
says the puerto rican girls from
the other side of the avenue
will push their strollers past us
says all winter long they have babies
says so they don't have to work
says makes me sick.

her mother through the window says
and why don't you work says
out on disability says
there's nothing wrong with you says
you just don't like people says
telling you what to do.

AND

where are you
and
how do we reach you
and
will we really be safe there
and
what if we get lost
and
what if we never arrive
and
what if we can't find our way back
and
what if there is nothing there
and
what if this is temporary
and
what if you're lying
and
what if we need to believe you anyway.

SECURE

there is a crack
between the door and jamb
through which the cold
enters.

THE

definite article determines thinglyness.

BLESSINGS

two   people
simultaneously   realize
the   permanence
of   the
isolate   separation
of   skin
    then
    kiss
    anyway.

OF

derived or coming from caused by away from
so as to be separated from the total or group comprising composed
or made associated with or adhering to possessing or having
centering upon or containing before or until
during or on a specified time set aside for specified as
or named or called characterized
or identified by with reference to.

LIBERTY

when they struck the bell it cracked in half
and fell from its high tower.

the crowd below once full of hope
never knew what hit them.

TO

future point
like toward
but closer.

OURSELVES

an hour sells

itself   as

time   less

pieces   of

a   life

there   is

not   much

left   for

us   to   do

together.

AND

there is always another
to connect to
another
to connect to
another
to connect to
another

in our galaxy alone
there are millions
of inhabitable planets

to connect to
another
to connect to
another
to connect to
another
there is always another.

OUR

to have something that can't be
held in two hands.

POSTERITY

while everyone was watching
he died and went to heaven.

DO

command this page into action.
give it purpose beyond its meaning.
perform this word.

ORDAIN

who selects the chosen
who says whom to trust and follow
who should save the rest of us
who is closest to god
and why.
and why.

AND

in 1972 everyone was doing it &
so you experimented with marijuana &
tried cocaine a couple of times &
sold some to a friend &
had different kinds of sex &
thought you got her pregnant &
liked kissing him &
copied the smart girl's final exam &
never told anyone & in 1976
graduated from college &
got a job at a major corporation & in 1978
learned to play golf &
got promoted & made more money &
wondered if it was worth it & in 1982
got married & bought a house &
a television for the living room & the kitchen & the bedroom &
subscribed to tv guide & time & in 1985
bought another new car &
thought about skipping out to drive west to see the ocean & in 1992
got promoted & made more money &
voted for conservative christian candidates &
went to strip clubs with co-workers for lap dances &
were never pulled over while you were driving drunk & in 1995
were eventually promoted to the top executive position &
began regularly compromising what you knew was right & in 1996
rationalized knowingly participating in racism & sexism & in 1997
moved jobs to third world countries &
looked only at bottom lines &
not human lives &
made more & more money & in 1998
exploited women & children's labor &

looked only at bottom lines &
not human lives &
made more & more money & in 1999
rationalized knowingly advertising lies &
looked only at bottom lines &
not human lives &
made more & more money & in the year 2000
started having trouble sleeping &
went dizzy with a pain in your chest &
wondered if there was a god &
were sorry for the person you became &
tried to ask for forgiveness &
didn't hear back.

ESTABLISH

measure
blueprint
lay it down
prop it up
maintain.

THIS

light:
a warm peach
melting.

CONSTITUTION

come to the blank page and write the first words
there in the blind dark of our history—
order sprung from the center of chaos.

FOR

prefix.
excessively
esp. with destructive or detrimental
effect:
forewarn.

THE

tall man stands so we can hear him
formally announce his story.

UNITED

in the better case
when one pledges
oneself to the other
the one is hoping
this can be true.
in the worse case
when one pledges
oneself to the other
the one knows
the inevitability of betrayal.

STATES

she says she says she says
sanity is south dakota
somewhere exactly in the middle

read this: the total length of the canadian boundary is 5,360 miles
and thought stars
read this: the total length of the mexican boundary is 2,013 miles
and thought stripes
read this: the total length of the atlantic coastline is 5,565 miles
and thought red
read this: the total length of the pacific and arctic coastline is 9,272 miles
and thought white
read this: the total length of the gulf of mexico coastline is 3,641 miles
and thought blue

this happened: south dakota pine ridge
but she says she says she says south dakota
sanity with a heart of river

this happened: south dakota rosebud
but she says she says she says south dakota
sanity with eyes of eagle

this happened: south dakota cheyenne river
but she says she says she says south dakota
sanity in arms of black hills

this happened: south dakota standing rock
but she says she says she says south dakota
sanity with thighs of timber and crows nest

this happened: south dakota wounded knee
but she says she says she says south dakota
sanity with a hunger for thunder and wind

this happened: south dakota mount rushmore
but she says she says she says south dakota

sanity in the center of caves

somewhere in the bad lands.

OF

a part, a piece
a story in succession
lineage.

AMERICA

an unsolved mathematical equation:
land plus people divided by people minus land
times ocean times forest times river.

escape and the delusion of discovery:
across the mad ocean to the rocky shore
step foot onto land call it yours.

promised land lemonade stand.
auction block stew pot.

the dreams:
of corn field wheat field tobacco field oil
of iron cage slave trade cotton plantation
of hog farm dairy farm cattle ranch range
of mississippi mason-dixon mountains
of territories salt lake lottery gold
of saw mill steel mill coal mine diamond.

topographic, economic
industry and war.

a box of longing
with fifty drawers.

BIOGRAPHY

Jen Benka has worked at social change organizations dedicated to ending homelessness and poverty, and ensuring women's economic equality and abortion rights. A native midwesterner, she now lives in New York City where she has co-organized events including a 24-hour marathon reading of the complete poems of Emily Dickinson and a protest poetry reading during the Republican National Convention. She works as the managing director of Poets & Writers.

Printed in the United States
By Bookmasters